T4-AQP-752

Written and illustrated
by George G. Rodgers

The C. R. Gibson Company
Norwalk, Connecticut

~Beyond the last mountain,
        across the endless tundra,
        to the edge of the polar sea,
I stalked the northern star.
Bullied by the wind,
        glared at by the sun,
        and burnt by the ice and snow,
I followed the azure glow . . .
Over granite fangs,
        deep into valleys of green silence,
        along the emotional cascades,
        and across the tidal flats,
I tracked this star called Polaris . . .
Day by day,
Season after season,
Until that final moment, cornered,
        no place left to go,
        my quarry turned,
        smiled . . . and spoke,
"Now, you belong to me."

~Last night the wolves called my name.
Not the name I now carry,
    but the one I was known by,
    a million winters ago.
How they knew it was me I am not sure,
    for I knew it not myself,
    but part of me knew,
    and part of me answered,
"Come, my brothers, let us run together,
Let us weave the patches of moonlight
    into a story, written on
    the fresh fallen snow.
For the world in sunlight to know
    that a band of brothers
    passed this place in time."

~To feel the cadence of the wings
     of the Canadians
      as they pencil-mark the sky.
To hear the snowflake fall.
To understand the gentle touch
     of a woman's hand.
To know the contentment
     of a kitten's purr.
As above, so below,
     I have felt the hand of God
     and I know self.

~There is a land that lies just beyond
        the horizons of my mind . . .
Sometimes in the purple mists of dawn,
        in that moment before I wake
        I see its golden peaks rising above the
        haze of everyday.
This land is to where I travel,
        guided by that tiny star within,
        and paced by the glass
        of falling sand.
Journey I must . . .
Find I will . . .
That far away country
        called, the seventh day.

~As above, so below.
When the twilight within
        becomes the dawn without.
To see for that brief moment,
        that short interlude,
        when the summer lightning reveals
        the world beyond evening sight.
As above, so below.
When the unknown becomes the known.
When the canvas of reality reveals
        the sketches from the studios of my mind,
Will the world of mind again, in time,
        touch that world of thine?

~The lances of my campfire keep the night
      at bay.
That flickering light that marks
      my presence on this earth,
      and gives a name to me.
Soon the embers will fade and the night
      will clothe me in its gown of
      abstraction.
Should the dawn find me gone
      from this forest and this earth,
Will anyone, aside from the deer and fox,
      know or remember that
      I passed by here once?

~I remember . . . in a land of many summers
　　　　ago . . . a small boy that spoke to
　　　　the land and the land spoke to him.
I remember . . . to be awakened
　　　　by the soft touch of the sun,
　　　　and to hear the meadowlark,
　　　　like the town crier,
　　　　singing of the new world.
I remember . . . feeling the healing touch
　　　　of the raindrops as they healed
　　　　the land and the souls of men.
I remember . . . feeling the lonely cry
　　　　of the loon, as he gathered
　　　　together all that could hear him,
　　　　into that one cloak of loneliness
　　　　that is common to
　　　　all living things.
I remember . . . standing at the shore of
　　　　the sea of grass and knowing the
　　　　stillness of the calm before the
　　　　storm, and watched the wind as it
　　　　raced ahead of the rain like a
　　　　giant broom sweeping ahead
　　　　before the scrubbing.
I remember . . . earthbound watching
　　　　the Canadians honk their way,
　　　　north or south and felt part of me
　　　　struggle to be with them.
I remember . . .

~This morning a very small chipmunk and I
     shared the same world,
     the same sun, and
     the same rocky ledge.
We did not speak, He and I.
We just looked and somehow knew
     that what was mine was his
     and what was his was mine.
I'm not quite sure, but somehow
     he looked quite familiar.
I think we have met before, He and I.
When I see him again I shall ask, maybe
     he will remember about He and I.

~I heard a man say today,
 "I shall help those people,
 I shall show them the way . . ."
Did I hear the voice of wisdom,
  or see a fool pick a flower?

~In the space allotted by a few grains of
 sand, measured by light and dark,
 boundries marked by spheres of nine.
In a form designed for government by
 the ordinance of nature, I strive
 to fulfill my charge, but where
 did I begin and where do I end?

Hence I have been allotted the sands of
nine times nine.
Is the full measure of light
and dark but one grain of sand?
Am I one or many?
From what distant shore did my voyage
depart and to what distant harbor
does home anchorage lie?
Were the shadows of today foretold
yesterday while I waited in
the anteroom for the passage of
the moon nine times?
Did I die to be born, and will I die
to be born again before my birth?
Where did I begin and where do I end?

~The wind is restless,
        no longer does it
        laugh among the leaves,
        as it did this summer.
Afraid to touch the earth, it races
        high in the tree tops,
        moaning and complaining.
It speaks of snow on the high
        far places, and it measures
        the time before it journeys south
        and leaves this land locked
        in a white silence.

~The whippoorwill shatters the silence.
Too early for night, too late for day,
        he wanders lost in the twilight,
        that world in between.
Who understands?
Does he speak of a place from whence
        he came, or does he speak of
        the place he journeys to?
Does he slip into this world through
        the crack between day and night?
Are his words "wait for me," or,
        "we will wait?"

~*I've stood on top of the world amidst*
　　　the endless harvest of snow and
　　　I knew that my being there was
　　　of no more importance than
　　　the smallest flake.
And I've heard the wild lonely cry of
　　　the sea gull and I've understood
　　　his song.
I've heard the whispering of my heart
　　　and the wind and each in his own way
　　　spoke the same.
I have seen the light go out in the eyes
　　　of men when they sold
　　　that part of them that said
　　　"I think" to the rest of the world
　　　for those coins of brass called
　　　"We think."

I have seen men reach for things
they could not have, and grown taller
for harvest.
I have found that secret place within
called the Tower of Babel, and
no man's tongue is stranger to me.
I've heard nature laugh when I discovered
that she created the strongest of
men the weakest, for the secret
wisdom of love belongs to another
called woman.
I have looked upon the face of God
and seen only the reflection
of my own inner self.
For my mother is the earth, my father
the sun, and I am brother to both
the tiger and man.
My kinsmen, the stars and the moon.
For one is one and each of us is part
of the other and I am not alone
except in a world of my own.

~The night erases the last of the amber
        from the sky, and my camp fire becomes
        only embers . . .
My thoughts now rest their wings, and I
        hear the cradlesong of the wind as it
        strums the boughs of pines . . .
Soon the Sirens of Sleep will lure me to
        the horizon of a new day . . .

~I am not my brother's keeper
I am my brother's brother . . .
In the evening I shall wait for him
       at the edge of the river . . .
To share the taste of bread and wine,
       and add to the warmth of the fire, the
       sound of voice . . .
But the shield he carries, and the trail
       he journeys is his own . . .
The wounds he suffers
       are his to survive . . .
The joys of the soul
       are his to cherish . . .
My wisdom, my vision are not threads
       strong enough to weave
       the fabric of his dream.
My hand shall not keep him
       from his journey . . .
I am not my brother's keeper,
I am my brother's brother.

~As I walked by the sea today
I felt the pulsating beat
The ebb and the flow
The rhythm common to all things,
        time and places
The pattern of day and night
The passage of the seasons
The pendulum of birth and death
The heartbeat of God
Life . . .

~My heart is a minstrel.
It sings the song of the voyageurs and
        the chants of the paddlemen
        as they fly the wild white water,
        and I have chased the sound.
It sings the songs of long ago,
        the memories of home and kin, womanly
        softness, but these fade away
        like the morning star before the
        approaching day.
It has thrilled me with the sounds of
        the lonely gull and the bugling elk,
        and it has blessed me with the laughter
        of children, and
        the hymns of the changing tides.
I know that when my journeys have
        shortened and I seek the quiet glen
        my heart will still hum reflections
        of a rhapsody written by God
The sound of life . . .

~Come, my brothers, suffer the pain
        of silence, and cross the frontier
        to another land . . .
Where the mountains and the valleys are
        beyond the measure of man . . .
The birthplace of tomorrow,
The beginning of all things,
The time and space just before
        the sound of now . . .

~I was there this morning when the sun
        lifted the edge of the sky and peeked in.
I guess he wanted to know if the place
        had been cleaned up
It had been . . .
        but he should have waited before
        he tracked all over the landscape . . .
It hadn't dried yet.

~I watched the world being torn apart
      today.
The courses of mighty rivers changed,
      mountains leveled and reshaped
      into towering dam and harbors.
Merchantmen and warships dispatched
      to distant shores.
The destiny of the world and history
      changed . . . by one small boy
      and one small mud puddle.

~I have been to the mountains and now I
        walk as a stranger in my own village.
The words I speak and the words I hear
        are manuscripts of silence.
Around me . . .
Faces, masquerades of yesteryear.
Voices, echoing the barking of
        false prophets.
Visions, fading dry, like the flower
        pressed in the book.
As the sound of the knell fades
        into time I gladly abdicate title
        or coin that clothes me in ritual
        for I must return to the mountains
        where eagle and I
        share the same sky . . .

~To track the eagle in flight
  To cage him in the air
  Is to capture him with your soul.

~Like a sound gently carried on the wind
I heard within a voice that seemed to
whisper my name.
A sound so faint that in my stillness
I hear only the sound
my mind fashions into an echo.
Was it my heart
or the wind that called my name?

~To all things there is a kinship.
That small touch of God called life.
The Grace that goes beyond color or
        place, and makes me part of all
        that exists.
In this vessel formed from the clay of
        the earth, there is
        the evolving thought of God.
For, not in the image of God,
        but in the vision of God
        was this vessel created,
        and the contours shaped
        by the land and time.
As above, so below, I bear
        the resemblance of all
        things created.
To know the land, and to see the seasons
Look upon my hands.
To see the land, and to know the seasons
Look upon my face.